THE BEST DESSERTS

51 Delicacies to Inspire, Delight
and Satisfy Even the Most
Discerning of Palates

Jason Pot

Additionally, the information in the following pages is intended only for informational purposes and should thus be thought of as universal. As befitting its nature, it is presented without assurance regarding its prolonged validity or interim quality. Trademarks that are mentioned are done without written consent and can in no way be considered an endorsement from the trademark holder.

Table of Contents

1.   Chocolate Cheesecake

Preparation Time: 25 mins, plus chilling, cooling, 2 hrs freezing and resting; no cook

Easy

Servings: 10-12

Ingredients:

For the biscuit base:

- 150g digestive biscuits (about 10)
- 1 tbsp caster sugar
- 45g butter, melted, plus extra for the tin

For the cheesecake:

- 150g dark chocolate
- 120ml double cream
- 2 tsp cocoa powder
- 200g full-fat cream cheese
- 115g caster sugar

Directions:

To make the biscuit base, crush the digestive biscuits with a rolling pin or blitz in a food processor, then tip into a bowl with the sugar and butter and stir to combine. Butter and line an 18cm springform tin and tip in the biscuit mixture, pushing it down with the back of a spoon. Chill in the fridge for 30 mins.

To make the cheesecake, melt the chocolate in short bursts in the microwave, then leave to cool slightly.

Whip the cream in a large bowl using an electric whisk until soft peaks form, then fold in the cocoa powder. Beat the cream cheese and sugar together, then fold in the cream mixture and the cooled chocolate. Spoon the cheesecake mixture over the biscuit base, levelling it out with the back of a spoon. Transfer to the freezer and freeze for 2 hrs, or until set. Remove from the tin and leave at room temperature to soften for about 20 mins before serving.

Nutrition: Per serving (12)

Kcal 296,   Fat: 20g,   Saturates: 12g,   Carbs: 25g,

Sugars: 19g,   Fibre: 2g,   Protein: 3g,   Salt: 0.4g

2.   Millionaire's Chocolate Brownie Tart

Preparation Time: 40 mins

Cooking Time:1 hr and 15 mins plus 2 hrs chilling

Servings: 10 – 12

Ingredients:

For the pastry:

- 175g plain flour, plus extra for dusting
- 85g icing sugar
- 50g cocoa powder
- 140g cold butter, cut into cubes
- 2 egg yolks, lightly beaten

For the filling:

- 150g butter, chopped
- 200g dark chocolate, broken into pieces
- 2 eggs
- 200g golden caster sugar
- 75g cocoa powder, plus extra to serve
- 18 caramel-filled chocolates

Directions:

To make the pastry, sift the flour, icing sugar and cocoa together into a bowl. Add the butter and rub it in with your fingers until the Mixture resembles breadcrumbs. Add the egg yolks and 3 tbsp ice-cold water, and continue to mix with your fingers until you have a soft dough. Alternatively, do this in a food processor by pulsing the ingredients together. Wrap the dough and chill for at least 1 hr. *Will keep chilled for up to two days*. Roll the dough out on a lightly floured surface to the thickness of a £1 coin, then use it to line a 23cm loose-bottomed tart tin, working the pastry to the edge and leaving some overhanging. Cover and put in the fridge to chill for a further hour. Heat the oven to 190C/170C fan/gas 5. Line the case with baking parchment, then fill with baking beans. Bake for 20 mins. Remove the baking beans and parchment, and bake for a further 15-20 mins, or until the base is crisp. Leave to cool completely. Once cooled, use a sharp knife to trim off the excess pastry and create a smooth edge. For the filling, melt the butter and dark chocolate together in a heatproof bowl set over a pan of simmering water, making sure the bowl doesn't touch the water. Stir until smooth, remove from the heat and leave to cool slightly.

Beat the eggs and sugar with an electric whisk in another bowl for 5-6 mins, or until thick and pale. Fold in the chocolate, then sift in the cocoa. Scatter the caramel chocolates over the base of the pastry case, then pour over the filling. Transfer the tart to a baking sheet and put in the oven (still set at 190C/170C fan/gas 5) for 20-25 mins, or until set and the top has formed a crust. Leave to cool to room temperature, then carefully remove from the tin and put on a serving plate. Dust with the extra cocoa and sprinkle over a little sea salt, if you like.

Nutrition: Per serving (12)

Kcal 528, Fat: 33g, Saturates: 20g, Carbs: 48g,

Sugars: 34g, Fibre: 4g, Protein: 7g, Salt: 0.5g

3.   Tiramisù Meringue Roulade

![hourglass] **Preparation Time:** 40 mins

![clock] **Cooking Time:** 20 mins

![chef hat] **Easy**

![cutlery] **Servings:** 8 – 10

Ingredients:

For the meringue:

- 4 large egg whites at room temperature
- 200g caster sugar
- icing sugar and cocoa powder, for dusting

For the mascarpone cream:

- 200ml double cream
- 50g dark brown soft sugar
- 150g mascarpone

- 3 tbsp masala coffee liqueur or normal coffee liqueur (optional)

For the coffee ganache:

- 4 tbsp instant coffee, dissolved in 50ml boiling water and left to cool slightly
- 100g dark chocolate, melted and left to cool slightly

Directions:

First, make the ganache. Whisk the coffee and melted chocolate together until you have a smooth, glossy mixture. Leave to cool and thicken, stirring occasionally. Heat the oven to 180C/160C fan/gas 4. Line a 23 x 32cm baking tray with baking parchment. For the meringue, beat the egg whites and a pinch of salt with an electric whisk until stiffened slightly. Add 1 tbsp of the caster sugar to the egg whites, then whisk again to stiff peaks. Repeat with the rest of the sugar, a spoonful at a time, until the mixture is thick and shiny. Spread evenly into the tray, then bake for 15-20 mins, or until crisp to the touch and lightly golden in places. Leave to cool completely. For the mascarpone cream filling, put the cream, sugar, mascarpone and liqueur, if using, in a medium bowl and whisk until thickened. To assemble, sift some icing sugar over a large sheet of baking parchment, then carefully flip the cooled meringue onto it. Lift off the tin and peel away the baking parchment. With a short end facing you, score a line 2cm into the edge of the meringue. Spread the ganache evenly over the meringue, then top with the cream, smoothing it with a palette knife, then carefully roll into a roulade, starting from the scored end and using the parchment to help.

Transfer to a serving plate and dust with cocoa powder.

Nutrition: Per serving (10)

Kcal 327,   Fat: 22g, Saturates: 14g,   Carbs: 29g,

Sugars: 28g,   Fibre: 1g,   Protein: 3g,   Salt: 0.1g

4.   Easy Cornflake Tart

Preparation Time: 20 mins

Cooking Time: 40 mins

Easy

Servings: 8-10

Ingredients:

- 320g ready-rolled shortcrust pastry
- plain flour, to dust
- 50g butter
- 125g golden syrup
- 25g light brown soft sugar
- 100g cornflakes
- 125g strawberry or raspberry jam
- custard, to serve

Directions:

Heat the oven to 180C/160C fan/gas 4. Unroll the pastry and briefly roll out on a lightly floured work surface until it's large enough to fit a 23cm loose-bottomed tart tin. Use the rolling pin to lift the pastry over the tin, then press into the corners and sides so the excess pastry hangs over the rim. Trim this away, leaving just a small amount of excess hanging over the rim. Line the pastry with baking parchment and fill with baking beans or uncooked rice. Bake for 15 mins.

Remove the parchment and beans, then bake for another 5-10 mins until just golden. Remove from the oven and trim any excess pastry from the edges using a serrated knife.

Heat the butter, syrup and sugar in a small pan with a pinch of salt, stirring frequently, until melted and smooth. Fold in the cornflakes to coat in the butter mixture. Spoon the jam into the cooked pastry base, then level the surface. Tip the cornflake mixture over the jam and gently press down until all of the jam is covered with a layer of the mixture. Return the tart to the oven and bake for another 5 mins until the cornflakes are golden and toasted. Leave to cool until just warm before slicing and serving with custard.

Nutrition: Per serving (10)

Kcal 305,   Fat: 14g,   Saturates: 6g,   Carbs: 41g,

Sugars: 21g,   Fibre: 1g,   Protein: 3g,   Salt: 0.49g

5.   Bakewell Tart

Preparation Time: 25 mins

Cooking Time: 55 mins plus chilling

Easy

Servings: 8

Ingredients:

- 250g plain flour , plus extra for rolling out
- ¼ tsp fine sea salt
- 2 tbsp icing sugar
- 140g cold butter , cubed
- 2 egg yolks , beaten
- cream or custard , to serve (optional)

For the filling:

- 100g salted butter , softened
- 100g caster sugar
- 50g ground almonds
- 1 tsp almond extract
- 2 medium eggs , beaten
- 3 tbsp raspberry jam
- 50g flaked almonds
- 80g icing sugar

Directions:

Heat the oven to 200C/180C fan/gas 6. To make the pastry, put the flour in a food processor along with the salt and icing sugar. Blitz to combine. Add the butter and pulse in short bursts until it's the texture of fine breadcrumbs. Mix 4 tbsp cold water with the beaten eggs and drizzle into the mixture, then quickly pulse to combine. Tip out the crumbly mixture onto a work surface, then form into a puck, cover and chill for 30 mins.

Roll the pastry out on a lightly floured surface to around 25cm, and to the thickness of a £1 coin. Line a 20cm fluted tart tin with the pastry, leaving the pastry to overhang. Add a large disc of baking parchment big enough to cover the edges, and some baking beans to weigh it down (use dried rice or lentils if you don't have baking beans). Bake for 15 mins, then remove the parchment and beans and bake for a further 7-10 mins or until the bottom is evenly cooked. Trim off any overhanging pastry with a serrated knife. For the filling, beat the butter and sugar until combined. Add the ground almonds, almond extract and eggs and beat for a further minute. Spread the jam over the pastry, then top with the almond filling. Scatter over the flaked almonds and bake for 25-30 mins until golden and firm. Leave to cool in the tin (or eat warm at this stage and leave out step 4).

Mix together the icing sugar and 1-2 tsp water and drizzle over the tart. Slice and serve with cream or custard, if you like.

Nutrition: Per serving

Kcal 572,   Fat: 35g,   Saturates: 17g,   Carbs: 55g,

Sugars: 31g,   Fibre: 1g,   Protein: 9g,   Salt: 0.77g

6.   Chocolate Orange Brownie Tart

Preparation Time: 20 mins

Cooking Time: 1 hr plus cooling

Easy

Servings: 6-8

Ingredients:

- 320g pack ready-made shortcrust pastry
- 120g dark chocolate, chopped
- 120g butter, cubed
- 2 eggs
- 80g golden caster sugar
- 80g light brown soft sugar
- 80g plain flour
- 1 orange, zested and juiced plus more zest to serve
- crème fraîche to serve

Directions:

Heat the oven to 180C/fan 160C/gas 4. Unravel the shortcrust pastry sheet and use to line a 20cm tart tin.

Press into the sides of the tin and loosely cut around the edges, leaving a little overhanging. Line the pastry with a scrunched-up piece of baking parchment, and fill with raw rice or baking beans. Bake for 15 mins, remove the paper and bake for another 5-10 mins until dry.

While the pastry is cooking, put the butter and chocolate into a heatproof bowl set over a pan of just-simmering water and melt together, stirring often. When melted, remove from the heat and leave to cool slightly. Add a pinch of salt if your butter is unsalted. Whisk together the eggs and sugars briefly in a bowl until combined, then stir in the melted chocolate and butter. Sieve over the flour and fold in until just combined. Stir in the orange juice and zest. Trim the edges of the pastry tart with a serrated knife to neaten, and spoon the brownie mixture into the middle. Smooth over with the back of a spoon or spatula, and bake for a further 30-35 mins until the top forms a crust, and the filling is no longer wet but slightly wobbly. Leave to cool for 15 mins before removing from the tin if serving warm, or serve at room temperature. Serve with a dollop of crème fraîche, and some more orange zest grated over. Keeps for 3 days in an airtight container.

Nutrition: Per serving (8)

Kcal 512,   Fat: 31g,   Saturates: 18g,   Carbs: 49g,

Sugars: 24g,   Fibre: 3g,   Protein: 6g,   Salt: 0.4g

7.   Boozy Baked Caramelised Bananas

Preparation Time: 10 mins

Cooking Time: 20 mins

Easy

Servings: 4

Ingredients:

- 6 ripe bananas, peeled and sliced in half lengthways
- 2 tbsp dark brown soft sugar
- 2 tbsp maple syrup
- 3-4 tbsp rum or whisky
- 40g pecans, toasted and chopped
- vanilla or salted caramel ice cream, to serve

Directions:

Heat the oven to 220C/200C fan/gas 8. Toss the banana halves in an ovenproof dish with the sugar, maple syrup and rum or whisky. Sprinkle with a small pinch of salt, if you like. Bake for 15 mins, then remove from the oven. Heat the grill to high and grill the bananas for 3-5 mins, or until bubbling and caramelised. Spoon the bananas into bowls and scatter over the pecans.Serve with ice cream, and any of the caramelised syrup from the dish drizzled over the top.

Nutrition: Per serving - Kcal 175, Fat:5g, Saturates:0.4g, Carbs:27g, Sugars: 24g, Fibre: 2g, Protein: 2g, Salt: 0.5g

8. Lemon & Elderflower Celebration Cake

Preparation Time: 45 mins

Cooking Time: 40 mins

More effort

Servings: 15-18

Ingredients:

- oil, for greasing
- 6 medium eggs
- 100g natural yoghurt
- 50ml milk
- 450g butter, softened
- 450g golden caster sugar
- 450g self-raising flour
- finely grated zest of 1 lemon, plus juice
- 3 tbsp elderflower cordial

For the icing:

- 250g butter, softened
- 300g full fat cream cheese
- 700g icing sugar
- finely grated zest of 1 lemon
- fresh flowers to decorate

Directions:

Heat oven to 160C/140C fan/gas 3. Grease and line the base and sides of 3 x 20cm cake tins with baking parchment. In a jug, whisk the eggs, yogurt and milk. Beat the butter and sugar together in a large bowl, using an electric hand whisk. When you have a light and fluffy mixture, add the flour, the liquid in the jug and the lemon zest. Mix again until smooth. Divide the cake mixture between the tins, level the surfaces and bake for 40 mins. Mix the lemon juice and elderflower cordial. When the cakes are cooked, poke all over the surface with a cocktail stick then spoon the lemon and elderflower syrup over the cakes. Leave to cool in the tins. Once cool, you can wrap in cling film and keep for 3 days before icing. To make the icing, beat the butter until smooth with an electric hand whisk. Add half the icing sugar, use a spatula to mash the mixture together (this will help to prevent an icing sugar cloud) then whisk again. Add the remaining icing sugar, cream cheese and lemon zest, mash again, then whisk again until smooth. Stack the cakes on a cake stand with plenty of icing between each layer. Pile most of the remaining icing on top, then use a palette knife to spread it across the top and down the sides, covering the cake in swirls (don't worry about it looking too perfect). Add the final bit of icing to the top and use it to cover any patches where the cake is poking through. Decorate with fresh flowers.

Nutrition: Per serving (18)

Kcal 715,   Fat: 38g,   Saturates: 24g,   Carbs: 86g,

Sugars: 67g,   Fibre: 1g,   Protein: 6g,   Salt: 1.13g

9.   Apple & Almond Crumble Pie

Preparation Time: 50 mins

Cooking Time: 40 mins plus standing

Easy

Servings: 6

Ingredients:

- 8 eating apples (Granny Smith or Braeburn work well)
- 50g golden caster sugar
- ½ tsp mixed spice
- 2 tbsp plain flour, plus extra for dusting
- 500g block shortcrust pastry
- 1 egg, beaten (optional)
- clotted cream, custard or ice cream, to serve

For the crumble:

- 50g plain flour
- 50g ground almonds
- 70g golden caster sugar
- 70g cold butter, cut into cubes
- 30g flaked almonds

Directions:

First, make the crumble. Tip the flour, ground almonds, sugar and a pinch of salt into a bowl, then rub in the butter with your fingers until the mix resembles breadcrumbs. Stir in the flaked almonds and chill until needed. *Can be prepared up to two days ahead and chilled.* Heat the oven to 200C/180C fan/gas 6 with a baking tray inside. Peel, core quarter and slice the apples, then tip into a bowl with the sugar, mixed spice and flour. Toss well and set aside. Roll the pastry out on a lightly floured surface until it's large enough to line a 20-22cm pie dish. Line the dish with the pastry, then trim and crimp the edge. Alternatively, re-roll the pastry trimmings into an 80cm-long strip, then cut into three thin, long strips, and arrange into a 1cm-wide plait. Arrange the plait around the edge of the dish, and brush with some beaten egg. Spoon the apples into the base, then scatter over the crumble. Bake on the hot tray for 35-40 mins until the topping is toasted and the pastry is deep golden. Leave to stand for 10 mins, then serve warm with cream, custard or ice cream.

Nutrition: Per serving

Kcal 765, Fat: 44g, Saturates: 17g, Carbs: 78g,

Sugars: 36g, Fibre:5g, Protein: 11g, Salt: 0.7g

10.   Banoffee Pie

 Preparation Time: 25 mins plus chilling

 Easy

 Servings: 8-10

Ingredients:

- 225g digestive biscuits
- 150g butter, melted
- 397g can caramel or 400g dulce de leche
- 3 small bananas, sliced
- 300ml double cream
- 1 tbsp icing sugar
- 1 square dark chocolate (optional)

Directions:

Crush the digestive biscuits, either by hand using a wooden spoon, or in a food processor, until you get fine crumbs, tip into a bowl. Mix the crushed biscuits

with the melted butter until fully combined.

Tip the mixture into a 23cm loose bottomed fluted tart tin and cover the tin, including the sides, with the biscuit in an even layer. Push down with the back of a spoon to smooth the surface and chill for 1 hr, or overnight.

Beat the caramel to loosen and spoon it over the bottom of the biscuit base. Spread it out evenly using

the back of a spoon or palette knife. Gently push the chopped banana into the top of the caramel until the base is covered. Put in the fridge. Whip the cream with the icing sugar until billowy and thick. Take the pie out of the fridge and spoon the whipped cream on top of the bananas. Grate the dark chocolate over the cream, if you like, and serve.

Nutrition: Per serving (10)

Kcal 518,   Fat: 36g,   Saturates: 21g,   Carbs:43g,

Sugars: 29g,   Fibre: 1g,   Protein:5g,   Salt:0.7g

11. Lemon & Raspberry Doughnut Pudding

Preparation Time: 15 mins

Cooking Time: 10 mins plus soaking

Easy

Servings: 8-10

Ingredients:

- butter, for the baking dish
- 8 raspberry jam doughnut
- 150g raspberries
- 500ml shop-bought fresh custard
- 250ml whole milk
- 150g lemon curd

Directions:

Heat the oven to 200C/180C fan/gas 6 and butter a 20 x 20cm baking dish. Quarter the raspberry jam doughnuts and arrange in overlapping layers in the prepared dish. Scatter over 100g raspberries.

Heat the custard with the milk until steaming, then whisk through the lemon curd. Pour the lemon custard over the doughnuts, then leave to soak for 30 mins, ensuring some of the doughnuts stick out so they'll crisp up when baked.

Scatter over another 50g raspberries and bake for 35-40 mins, or until golden brown and just set.

Nutrition: Per serving (10)

Kcal 314,   Fat: 12g,   Saturates:5g,   Carbs:46g,

Sugars: 27g,   Fibre:2g,   Protein: 6g,   Salt: 0.7g

12. Cinnamon Apple Turnover

Preparation time: 10 minutes

Cooking time: 25 minutes

Servings: 4 to 6

Ingredients:

- 1 large Granny Smith apple, peeled, cored, and diced
- ½ teaspoon cornstarch
- ¼ teaspoon cinnamon
- Dash ground nutmeg
- ¼ cup brown sugar
- ¼ cup applesauce
- ¼ teaspoon vanilla extract
- 1 tablespoon butter, melted
- 1 sheet of puff pastry, thawed
- Whipped cream or vanilla ice cream, to Serving

Directions:

Preheat the oven to 400°F. Prepare a baking sheet by spraying it with non-stick cooking spray or using a bit of oil on a paper towel. In a mixing bowl, mix together the apples, cornstarch, cinnamon, nutmeg, and brown sugar. Stir to make sure the apples are well covered with the spices. Then stir in the applesauce and the vanilla. Lay out your puff pastry and cut it into squares. You should be able to make 4 or 6 depending on how big you want your turnovers to be and how big your pastry is. Place some of the apple mixture in the center of each square and fold the corners of the pastry up to make a pocket. Pinch the edges together to seal. Then brush a bit of the melted butter over the top to give the turnovers that nice brown color. Place the filled pastry onto the prepared baking pan and transfer it to the preheated oven. Bake 20–25 minutes, or until they become a golden brown in color. Serve with whipped cream or vanilla ice cream.

Nutrition:

Calories: 332,   Fat: 24 g,   Carbs: 65 g,

Protein: 76 g,   Sodium: 767 mg

13.   Cherry Chocolate Cobbler

Preparation time: 10 minutes

Cooking time: 45 minutes

Servings: 8

Ingredients:

- 1½ cups all-purpose flour
- ½ cup sugar
- 2 teaspoons baking powder
- ½ teaspoon salt
- ¼ cup butter
- 6 ounces semisweet chocolate morsels
- ¼ cup milk 1 egg, beaten
- 21 ounces cherry pie filling
- ½ cup finely chopped nuts

Directions:

Preheat the oven to 350°F. Combine the flour, sugar, baking powder, salt, and butter in a large mixing bowl. Use a pastry blender to cut the mixture until there are lumps the size of small peas. Melt the chocolate morsels. Let cool for approximately 5 minutes, then add the milk and egg and mix well. Beat into the flour mixture, mixing completely. Spread the pie filling in a 2-quart casserole dish. Randomly drop the chocolate batter over the filling and then sprinkle with nuts. Bake for 40–45 minutes. Serve with a scoop of vanilla ice cream if desired.

Nutrition:

Calories: 243,   Fat: 41 g,   Carbs: 75 g,   Protein:67 g,
Sodium: 879 mg

14.   Chocolate Pecan Pie

Preparation time: 10 minutes

Cooking time: 50 minutes

Servings: 8

Ingredients:

- 3 eggs
- ½ cup sugar
- 1 cup corn syrup
- ½ teaspoon salt
- 1 teaspoon vanilla extract
- ¼ cup melted butter
- 1 cup pecans
- 3 tablespoons semisweet chocolate chips
- 1 unbaked pie shell

Directions:

Preheat the oven to 350°F. Beat together the eggs and sugar in a mixing bowl, then add the corn syrup, salt, vanilla, and butter. Put the chocolate chips and pecans inside the pie shell and pour the egg mixture over the top. Bake for 50–60 minutes or until set.

Serve with vanilla ice cream.

Nutrition:

Calories: 465,   Fat: 76 g, Carbs: 37 g, Protein: 97 g,

Sodium: 4461 mg

15. Baked Apple Dumplings

Preparation time: 20 minutes

Cooking time: 40 minutes

Servings: 2 to 4

Ingredients:

- 1 (17½ ounce) package frozen puff pastry, thawed
- 1 cup sugar
- 6 tablespoons dry breadcrumbs
- 2 teaspoons ground cinnamon
- 1 pinch ground nutmeg
- 1 egg, beaten
- 4 Granny Smith apples, peeled, cored and halved Vanilla ice cream for serving

Icing:

- 1 cup confectioners' sugar
- 1 teaspoon vanilla extract
- 3 tablespoons milk
- Pecan Streusel
- ⅔ Cup chopped toasted pecans
- ⅔ Cup packed brown sugar
- ⅔ Cup all-purpose flour
- 5 tablespoons melted butter

Directions:

Preheat the oven to 425°F. When the puff pastry has completely thawed, roll out each sheet to measure 12 inches by 12 inches. Cut the sheets into quarters. Combine the sugar, breadcrumbs, cinnamon and nutmeg together in a small bowl. Brush one of the pastry squares with some of the beaten egg. Add about 1 tablespoon of the breadcrumb mixture on top, and then add half an apple, core side down, over the crumbs. Add another tablespoon of the breadcrumb mixture. Seal the dumpling by pulling up the corners and pinching the pastry together until the seams are totally sealed. Repeat this process with the remaining squares. Assemble the ingredients for the pecan streusel in a small bowl. Grease a baking sheet or line it with parchment paper. Place the dumplings on the sheet and brush them with a bit more of the beaten egg. Top with the pecan streusel.

Bake for 15 minutes, then reduce heat to 350°F and bake for 25 minutes more or until lightly browned. Make the icing by combining the confectioners' sugar, vanilla, and milk until you reach the proper consistency.

When the dumplings are done, let them cool to room temperature and drizzle them with icing before serving.

Nutrition:

Calories: 145,   Fat: 57 g,   Carbs: 87 g,

Protein: 66.9 g,   Sodium: 529 mg

16. Peach Cobbler

Preparation time: 10 minutes

Cooking time: 45 minutes

Servings: 4

Ingredients:

- 1¼ cups Bisquick
- 1 cup milk
- ½ cup melted butter
- ¼ teaspoon nutmeg
- ½ teaspoon cinnamon
- Vanilla ice cream, for serving

Filling:

- 1 (30-ounce) can peaches in syrup, drained
- ¼ cup sugar
- Topping
- ½ cup brown sugar
- ¼ cup almond slices
- ½ teaspoon cinnamon
- 1 tablespoon melted butter

Directions:

Preheat the oven to 375°F. Grease the bottom and sides of an 8×8-inch pan. Whisk together the Bisquick, milk, butter, nutmeg, and cinnamon in a large mixing bowl. When thoroughly combined, pour into the greased baking pan. Mix together the peaches and sugar in another mixing bowl. Put the filling on top of the batter in the pan. Bake for about 45 minutes. In another bowl, mix together the brown sugar, almonds, cinnamon, and melted butter. After the cobbler has cooked for 45 minutes, cover evenly with the topping and bake for an additional 10 minutes.

Serve with a scoop of vanilla ice cream.

Nutrition:

Calories: 168,   Fat: 76 g,   Carbs: 15 g,

Protein: 78.9 g,   Sodium: 436 mg

17.   Royal Dansk Butter Cookies

Preparation time: 15 minutes

Cooking time: 25 minutes

Servings: 10

Ingredients:

- 120g cake flour, sifted
- ½ teaspoon vanilla extract
- 25g powdered sugar
- 120g softened butter, at room temperature
- A pinch of sea salt, approximately ¼ teaspoon

Directions:

Using a hand mixer; beat the butter with sugar, vanilla & salt until almost doubled in mass & lightened to a yellowish-white in color, for 8 to 10 minutes, on low to middle speed. Scrape the mixture from the sides of your bowl using a rubber spatula. Sift the flour x 3 times & gently fold in until well incorporated. Transfer the mixture into a sheet of plastic wrap, roll into a log & cut a hole on it; place it into the piping bag attached with nozzle flower tips 4.6cm/1.81" x 1.18". Pipe each cookie into 5cm wide swirls on a parchment paper-lined baking tray. Cover & place them in a freezer until firm up, for 30 minutes. Preheat your oven to 300 F in advance. Once done, bake until the edges start to turn golden, for 20 minutes. Let completely cool on the cooling rack before serving. Store them in an airtight container.

Nutrition:

Calories: 455,   Fat: 67 g,   Carbs: 12. 8 g,

Protein: 66.3 g,   Sodium: 552 mg

18. Campfire S'mores

Preparation time: 15 minutes

Cooking time: 40 minutes

Servings: 9

Ingredients:

- Graham Cracker Crust
- 2 cups graham cracker crumbs
- ¼ cup sugar
- ½ cup butter
- ½ teaspoon cinnamon
- 1 small package brownie mix (enough for an 8×8-inch pan), or use the brownie ingredients listed below.

Brownie Mix:

- ½ cup flour
- ⅓ Cup cocoa
- ¼ teaspoon baking powder
- ¼ teaspoon salt
- ½ cup butter
- 1 cup sugar
- 1 teaspoon vanilla
- 2 large eggs
- S'mores Topping

- 9 large marshmallows

- 5 Hershey candy bars

- 4½ cups vanilla ice cream

- ½ cup chocolate sauce

Directions:

Preheat the oven to 350°F. Mix together the graham cracker crumbs, sugar, cinnamon and melted butter in a medium bowl. Stir until the crumbs and sugar have combined with the butter. Line an 8×8-inch baking dish with parchment paper, make sure to use enough so that you'll be able to lift the baked brownies out of the dish easily. Press the graham cracker mixture into the bottom of the lined pan. Place pan in the oven to prebake the crust a bit while you are making the brownie mixture. Melt the butter over medium heat in a large saucepan and then stir in the sugar and vanilla. Whisk in the eggs one at a time. Then whisk in the dry ingredients, followed by the nuts. Mix until smooth. Take the crust out of the oven, pour the mixture into it, and bake for 23–25 minutes. When brownies are done, remove from oven and let cool in the pan. After the brownies have cooled completely, lift them out of the pan using the edges of the parchment paper. Be careful not to crack or break the brownies. Cut into individual slices. When you are ready to Serve, place a marshmallow on top of each brownie and broil in the oven until the marshmallow starts to brown. You can also microwave for a couple of seconds, but you won't get the browning that you would in the broiler.

Remove from the oven and top each brownie with half of a Hershey bar. Serve with ice cream and a drizzle of chocolate sauce.

Nutrition:

Calories: 187,   Fat: 18.9 g,   Carbs: 56.6 g,

Protein: 65.2,   Sodium: 552 mg

19. Banana Pudding

Preparation time: 15 minutes

Cooking time: 1 hour and 30 minutes

Servings: 8 to 10

Ingredients:

- 6 cups milk
- 5 eggs, beaten
- ¼ teaspoon vanilla extract
- 1⅛ cups flour
- 1½ cups sugar
- ¾ pound vanilla wafers
- 3 bananas, peeled
- 8 ounces Cool Whip or 2 cups of whipped cream

Directions:

In a large saucepan, heat the milk to about 170°F. Mix the eggs, vanilla, flour, and sugar together in a large bowl. Very slowly add the egg mixture to the warmed milk and cook until the mixture thickens to a custard consistency. Layer the vanilla wafers to cover the bottom of a baking pan or glass baking dish. You can also use individual portion dessert dish or glasses. Layer banana slices over the top of the vanilla wafers. Be as liberal with the bananas as you want.

Layer the custard mixture on top of the wafers and bananas. Move the pan to the refrigerator and cool for 1½ hours. When ready to Serve, spread Cool Whip (or real whipped cream, if you prefer) over the top. Garnish with banana slices and wafers if desired.

Nutrition:

Calories: 166,   Fat: 56 g,   Carbs: 78.9 g,

Protein: 47.8 g,   Sodium: 578 mg

20. Chocolate Cherry Cobbler

Preparation time: 10 minutes

Cooking time: 45 minutes

Servings: 8

Ingredients:

- 1 can (21 oz.) cherry pie filling
- 1½ cups flour
- ½ cup sugar
- 2 tsp. baking powder
- ½ tsp. salt
- ¼ cup (1/2 stick) cold butter1 egg
- 1 cup (a 6 oz. bag) chocolate chips
- ¼ cup evaporated milk
- ½ cup slivered almonds

Directions:

Preheat oven to 350 degrees F. You will need a 1½ to 2-quart baking dish (I used a 1.5 QT oval).

Mix flour, sugar, salt & baking powder in a medium bowl. Cut butter into chunks and add to the flour mixture. Cut in butter until the mixture resembles small peas. Set aside. Spread cherry pie filling in the bottom of a 1.5 to 2-quart baking dish. Set aside. Melt chocolate chips either in the microwave or stovetop. Stir frequently until the chips are all melted, and mixture is smooth. Cool for about 5 minutes. Add evaporated milk and egg to melted chocolate chips. Stir until well blended. Add the chocolate mixture to the flour mixture. Mix very well. Drop randomly on top of cherry filling in baking dish. Sprinkle with the almonds. Bake at 350 degrees F for 40-45 minutes. Serve warm with ice cream, whipped cream, or cream.

Nutrition:

Calories: 460,   Carbs: 65g,   Protein: 6g,

Fat: 19g,   Saturated Fat: 9g,   Sugar: 20g,

Fiber: 3g, Cholesterol: 37mg, Sodium: 225mg, Potassium: 396mg

21.   Apple Dumpling Bake

Preparation time: 15 minutes

Cooking time: 35 minutes

Servings: 8

Ingredients:

- 2 medium Granny Smith apples
- 2 tubes (8 ounces each) refrigerated crescent rolls
- 1 cup sugar
- 1/3 cup butter, softened
- 1/2 teaspoon ground cinnamon
- 3/4 cup Mountain Dew soda
- Vanilla ice cream

Directions:

Preheat oven to 350°. Peel, core and cut each apple into 8 wedges. Unroll both tubes of crescent dough; separate each into 8 triangles. Wrap a triangle around each wedge. Place in a greased 13x9-in. baking dish. In a bowl, mix sugar, butter, and cinnamon until blended, sprinkle over dumplings. Slowly pour soda around the rolls (do not stir). Bake, uncovered, until golden brown and apples are tender, 35-40 minutes, serve warm with ice cream.

Nutrition:

Calories: 414,   Fat: 20g,   Saturated fat: 9g, Cholesterol: 20mg, Carbohydrate: 510mg, Sodium: 510mg, Fiber: 1g,   Sugar: 510mg,

22. Homemade Corn Muffins with Honey Butter

Preparation time: 20 minutes

Cooking time: 20 minutes

Servings: 16

Ingredients:

- 1/4 cup butter, softened
- 1/4 cup reduced-fat cream cheese
- 1/2 cup sugar 2 large eggs
- 1-1/2 cups fat-free milk
- 1-1/2 cups all-purpose flour
- 1-1/2 cups yellow cornmeal
- 4 teaspoons baking powder
- 3/4 teaspoon salt

Honey Butter:

- 1/4 cup butter, softened

- 2 tablespoons honey

Directions:

In a large bowl, cream the butter, cream cheese, and sugar until light and fluffy. Add eggs, one at a time, beating well after each addition. Stir in the milk. Combine the flour, cornmeal, baking powder and salt; add to creamed mixture just until moistened. Coat muffin cups with cooking spray; fill three-fourths full of batter. Bake at 400° for 18-22 minutes or until a toothpick inserted in the center comes out clean. Cool for 5 minutes before removing from pans to wire racks.

Beat butter and honey until blended; Serve with warm muffins.

Nutrition:

Calories: 198, Fat: 7g, Cholesterol: 45mg, Sodium: 285mg, Carbohydrate: 29g, Protein: 4g

23. Peach Cobbler with Almond Crumble Topping

Preparation time: 15 minutes

Cooking time: 1 hour

Servings: 6 to 9

Ingredients:

Batter:

- 1 cup cracker barrel pancake mix (can substitute but I would not)
- 1 cup milk
- ½ cup melted butter
- ¼ teaspoon nutmeg
- ½ teaspoon cinnamon

Filling:

- 2 (15 ounce) cans peach slices in heavy syrup or (15 ounce) cans diced peaches in heavy syrup
- ¼ cup sugar

Topping:

- ½ cup brown sugar
- 1/8 cup flour
- ½ teaspoon cinnamon
- 1 tablespoon softened butter

- Sliced almonds

Directions:

Mix all batter Ingredients in a bowl with whisk until well incorporated and light. Pour into non greased 8 x 8 baking pan. Drain peaches of syrup except for about a tablespoon of juice in each can and mix with sugar until it has dissolved. Pour over batter but do not mix -- batter will rise over peaches and juices on its own. Mix all topping Ingredients with hands slightly breaking up almonds as you incorporate. Do not place on cobbler yet as the almonds will burn! That step will come later. Place into 375-degree oven for 45 minutes. Then, while leaving cobbler in oven, place crumble topping over cobbler and bake another 10-15 minutes. Watch carefully so that nuts do not burn. Serve while still a little warm with some cinnamon ice cream and enjoy!

Nutrition:

Calories:475.1,   TotalCarbohydrate: 72.2g,

Total Fat: 20.1g,   Cholesterol: 56mg,   Sugars: 46.9g,

Sodium: 449mg,   Dietary Fiber:2.6g,   Protein: 4.8 g

24.   Strawberry Shortcake

Preparation time: 10 minutes

Cooking time: 10 minutes

Servings: 8

Ingredients:

- 1 pre-made pound cake
- 1-pint frozen sweetened strawberries
- 4 scoops premium vanilla ice cream
- 1 can whipped cream
- Scratch 4 scoops vanilla ice cream
- 1 homemade pound cake
- 1-pound Fresh strawberries
- 1-pint whipped cream

Directions:

Quick and Easy Assembly Assemble strawberry shortcake by cutting two slices of the pound cake and then slicing those in half. In a bowl, place the 4 pieces of pound cake across from each other. Spoon defrosted strawberries onto cake; add one scoop of vanilla ice cream and top with whipped cream. While the Cracker Barrel may use frozen strawberries, I really like fresh ones much more. I think you can jazz up this recipe by using fresh strawberries, fresh whipped cream, and if you are up to it, a homemade pound cake. From Scratch Method Prepare the strawberries several hours ahead of time by cleaning them, slicing them, and placing them into a bowl. Add about 1 tablespoon of superfine sugar, if available, to the strawberries and mix well. Place strawberries in the refrigerator. The sugar will help to make the strawberries juicy. Whip the whipping cream with a mixer until firm. You may want to add a touch of vanilla to this for some extra flavor. When you are ready to serve the shortcakes, follow the Instructions above.

Nutrition:

Calories: 542, Carbohydrates: 77g, Fat: 22g, Protein:9g, Saturated Fat:13g, Cholesterol:150mg, Sodium: 460mg, Potassium: 469mg, Fiber: 3g, Sugar: 51g

25. Absolutely Fabulous Greek/House Dressing

Preparation Time: 10 minutes

Cooking time: 10 minutes

Servings: 1

Ingredients:

- 1/3 cup garlic powder
- 1/3 cup dried oregano
- 1/3 cup dried basil
- 1/4 cup pepper
- 1/4 cup salt
- 1/4 cup onion powder
- 1/4 cup Dijon-style mustard
- 2 quarts red wine vinegar

Directions:

Combine Dijon-style mustard, olive oil, onion powder, garlic powder, salt, oregano, pepper, and basil in a big container. Mix in vinegar forcefully until well combined. Cover tightly and store at room temperature.

Nutrition:

Calories: 104,   Total Carbohydrate: 2.1 g,   Cholesterol: 0 mg,

Total Fat: 10.8g,   Protein: 0.2 g,   Sodium: 13 mg

26.   Fried Apples

Preparation Time: 10 minutes

Cooking Time: 20 minutes

Servings: 8

Ingredients:

- 6 Granny Smith Apples - peeled and sliced (10 slices per apple)
- ¼ Cup of Margarine
- ¼ Cup Brown Sugar
- ⅛ Teaspoon Salt
- ⅛ Teaspoon of Nutmeg
- 1 Teaspoon of Cinnamon
- 1 Teaspoon of Lemon Juice

Directions:

Melt margarine in a large skillet over medium/low heat. Place apple slices in skillet - try and make it even. Pour lemon juice on top -- try and get the juice on as many apples as possible. Sprinkle brown sugar + Salt onto the apples. Cover and cook for 15 minutes - turn over once. Make sure the apples are tender. Sprinkles Cinnamon and Nutmeg on Top of Apples

Nutrition:

Calories:78, Carbohydrates:7g, Fat:5g, Protein: 0g,

Saturated Fat: 3g, Sugar: 6g, Fiber: 0g,

Sodium: 88mg, Cholesterol: 15mg, Potassium: 9mg

27. Old Country Store Double Fudge Coca Cola Cake

🕰 **Preparation Time:** 10 minutes

🕐 **Cooking Time**: 30 minutes

🍴 **Servings**: 24

Ingredients:

Cake:

- 1 cup Coca-Cola
- 1/2 cup oil
- 1/2 cup or 1 stick margarine
- 3 tablespoons of cocoa
- 2 cups sugar
- 2 cups all-purpose flour
- 1/2 teaspoon salt
- 2 eggs
- 1/2 cup buttermilk
- 1 teaspoon baking soda
- 1 teaspoon vanilla

Frosting:

- 1/2 cup or 1 stick of margarine
- 3 tablespoons cocoa
- 6 tablespoons cream or milk

- 1 teaspoon vanilla
- 1/2 to 1 cup chopped pecans
- 1-pound confectioners' sugar

Directions:

Cake:

In a saucepan, bring Coca-Cola, oil, margarine, and cocoa to a boil. Mix the sugar, flour, and salt, pour into the boiling liquid, and beat well. Add the eggs, buttermilk, baking soda, and vanilla and beat well. Pour into a greased and floured sheet cake pan and bake at 350 degrees for 20-25 minutes.

Frosting:

In a saucepan, combine the margarine, cocoa, and cream or milk and heat until the butter melts. Beat in the remaining ingredients. Spread on the hot cake. Cool and cut.

Nutrition:

Calories: 334,   Carbohydrates: 46g,

Protein: 2g,   Fat: 16g, Saturated Fat: 5g, Cholesterol: 34mg,   Sodium: 175mg,

Potassium: 65mg,   Fiber: 1g,   Sugar: 36g

28.   Pumpkin Custard N' Ginger Snaps

⧖ **Preparation Time:** 30 minutes

🕐 **Cooking Time**: 35 minutes

✂ **Servings:** 8

Ingredients:

- 8 egg yolks
- 1 3/4 cup pure pumpkin puree - 1 (15 ounce) can of pure pumpkin
- 1 3/4 cup heavy whipping cream
- 1/2 cup granulated sugar
- 1 1/2 teaspoon pumpkin pie spice
- 1 teaspoon vanilla
- 1 cup ginger snap cookies and about
- 8 ginger snap cookies that are whole
- 1 tablespoon melted butter

- 1 cup heavy whipping cream
- 1 tablespoon granulated sugar if you have extra fine sugar this is best
- 1/2 teaspoon pumpkin pie spice

Directions:

Preheat oven to 350 degrees. Crack open 8 eggs and separate the whites from the yolks. In a medium-sized glass bowl add egg yolks and whisk until they are creamy. Add pumpkin, 1/2 cup sugar, vanilla, 1 3/4 cups of heavy cream, and pumpkin pie spice and combine until all are incorporated. Cook custard mixture in a double boiler, and stir until custard has thickened, and a spoon remains coated when inserted into the custard. Pour custard into either 8 custard dishes, or an 8 x 8 baking dish. Bake custard for about 30-35 minutes or until a spoon is inserted comes out clean. Halfway through the baking process combine the 1 cup gingersnaps and 1 tablespoon melted butter, and sprinkle the crumb mixture over the custard while it is baking by removing the dishes from the oven, adding gingersnap crumb mixture and returning the dishes to the oven to finish baking. If you are using small individual custard dishes check the custard at 20-25 minutes. Allow the custard to cool to room temperature. Just before serving mix the pumpkin pie spice-infused whipped cream by whisking together the 1 cup whipping cream, 1 tablespoon granulated sugar, and 1/4 teaspoon pumpkin pie spice until the whipped cream is thickened.

Nutrition:

Sodium: 126mg, Sugar: 18g

Calories: 487,   Carbohydrates: 32g,   Fat: 38g,   Protein: 5g,

Potassium: 240mg, Fiber: 1g, Saturated Fat: 21g, Cholesterol: 311mg,

29.   Old Country Store Carrot Cake

Preparation Time: 20 minutes

Cooking Time: 50 minutes

Servings: 24

Ingredients:

Cake ingredients:

- 3/4 cup finely chopped English walnuts
- 2 cups finely shredded carrots
- 8 ounces crushed pineapple do not drain
- 1/2 cup finely shredded coconut
- 1/2 cup raisins that have been soaked in water until plump and then drained
- 1 1/4 cup vegetable oil
- 1 1/2 cup sugar
- 1/2 cup brown sugar
- 3 eggs
- 3 cups all-purpose flour
- 2 teaspoons baking powder
- 2 teaspoons baking soda
- 2 teaspoons vanilla
- 2 teaspoons ground cinnamon
- 1 teaspoon ground nutmeg

- 1/2 teaspoon ground cloves
- 1/2 teaspoon salt

Cream Cheese Frosting:

- 8 ounces cream cheese
- 4 ounces butter at room temperature
- 1 teaspoon vanilla
- 2 cups powdered sugar
- 1/2 cup chopped pecans for garnish

Directions:

For the Cake:

Mix together flour, baking powder, baking soda, salt, cinnamon, nutmeg, and cloves. Set aside. In a large bowl, mix the vegetable oil, sugars, vanilla, and eggs until smooth and fluffy. Add pineapple, walnuts, coconut, carrots, and raisins and blend well. Gradually add flour mixture a half at a time until blended through. Pour batter into a greased and floured 9x13 inch pan and bake at 350 degrees for about 40-50 minutes. Test with a toothpick for doneness. When cool, frost with cream cheese frosting.

For the Cream Cheese Frosting:

Blend cream cheese and butter until light and fluffy. Add vanilla and a little of the powdered sugar at a time until all has been blended well. Turn mixer on high and beat until frosting is light and fluffy. Spread frosting over the cooled cake and sprinkle with pecans.

Nutrition:

Calories: 318, Carbohydrates: 45g,

Fat: 14g, Protein: 4g, Saturated Fat: 6g,

Sugar: 29g, Cholesterol: 41mg, Sodium: 222mg, Potassium: 182 mg,

Fiber: 1g

30.   Cinnabon Cinnamon Swirl Cheesecake

Preparation Time: 25 minutes

Cooking Time: 1 hour & 40 minutes

Servings: 8

Ingredients:

- 17 rectangles graham crackers
- 1 tablespoon butter flavoring
- 3 tablespoons cornstarch
- 1 ⅓ cups raw sugar
- 5 tablespoon vegan margarine, melted
- ⅔ cup vegan sour cream
- 3 packages of vegan cream cheese, at room temperature (8 ounce)
- 1 teaspoon lemon zest
- 2 tablespoon vanilla nut & butter flavoring
- 1 tablespoon almond milk
- 3 tablespoon raw sugar
- ½ cup firm tofu
- 2 teaspoon cinnamon
- ½ cup dark brown sugar
- reserved 3/8 cup of the batter

Directions:

Generously grease the bottom & sides of a spring form pan then line the bottom with wax paper and preheat your oven to 350 F. Form the crust by melting the margarine; add in the butter flavoring, mix well & set aside. Now, grind the graham crackers in a food processor and then add in the sugar, process for on high speed for a minute. Combine the butter mixtures together with graham cracker in a medium bowl until incorporated well. Press the mixture to the bottom of the spring form pan; set aside.

Prepare the batter by blending ⅓ cup of the sugar and cornstarch with a package of the cream cheese for a couple of minutes on low. Stop; scrape down the sides of your bowl and then slowly add in the leftover cream cheese; do not forget to scrape the sides of your bowl down, as required. Combine the leftover sugar with lemon zest. Increase the speed to medium & add lemon sugar into the cream cheese mixture. Add in the vanilla; scrape the sides & set aside. Combine tofu with almond milk in a blender or food processor until completely smooth. Mix in tofu mixture into the batter on medium speed. Add in the sour cream; mix well & scrape the sides again.

Reserve approximately 3/8 cup of the batter for swirl mixture. Pour the leftover batter into the prepared pan over the crust; set aside. For swirl mixture take the kept-aside batter together with cinnamon & brown sugar; combine well. Scoop a few tablespoons full of the cinnamon mixture over the cheesecake; pressing it down gently with a spoon. Swirl the cinnamon using a knife tip to. Bake in the preheated oven for 60 to 75 minutes. Let cool for a few hours. Cover & let refrigerate for 4 hours more. Garnish with the brown rice syrup and chopped pecans; serve immediately & enjoy.

Nutrition:

Calories:1370,   Total Fat:85g,   Dietary Fiber: 2g,

Sugars: 120g,   Protein: 10g,   Cholesterol: 275mg,

Sodium: 710mg,   Total Carbohydrate: 141g,

31.   Lemon Cheesecake

Preparation Time: 20 mins

Cooking Time: 5 mins, plus chilling

Serves: 6

Ingredients:

- 110g digestive biscuits
- 50g butter
- 25g light brown soft sugar
- 350g mascarpone
- 75g caster sugar
- 1 lemon, zested
- 2-3 lemons, juiced (about 90ml)

Directions:

Crush the digestive biscuits in a food bag with a rolling pin or in the food processor. Melt the butter in a saucepan, take off heat and stir in the brown sugar and biscuit crumbs. Line the base of a 20cm loose bottomed cake tin with baking parchment. Press the biscuit into the bottom of the tin and chill in the fridge while making the topping. Beat together the mascarpone, caster sugar, lemon zest and juice, until smooth and creamy. Spread over the base and chill for a couple of hours.

Nutrition: Kcal 470,   Fat: 37g,   Saturates: 23g,   Salt: 0.5g
Carbs: 31g,   Sugars: 22g,   Fibre: 1g,   Protein: 4g,

32.   Berry Brulée

Preparation Time: 10 mins

Cooking time: 20 mins, plus chilling

Serves: 6

Ingredients:

- 50g pudding rice
- 140g cherries , redcurrants or blueberries
- 4 tbsp cassis liquer
- 1 vanilla pod , split
- 568ml pot double cream
- 6 medium eggs
- 2 tbsp golden caster sugar

For the topping:

- 85g golden caster sugar

Directions:

Cook the rice according to pack instructions. Drain and cool. Divide the fruit between 6 x 150ml ramekin dishes, drizzle the cassis over and set to one side. Scrape the seeds from the vanilla pod and put in a pan with the cream and the empty pod. Bring to the boil, then remove from the heat and leave for 5 mins. Remove and discard the vanilla pod. Mix the egg yolks and sugar in a large bowl. Stir the cream into the egg. Return to the pan and cook over a low heat, stirring constantly, until it thickens. Stir the cooked rice into the custard mixture. Ladle into the ramekins and leave in the fridge for 6 hrs. Sprinkle sugar over the tops and caramelise with a blow torch or under a very hot grill until it turns dark brown. Let it cool and harden before serving.

Nutrition:

Kcal 669,   Fat: 56g,   Saturates: 30g,

Carbs: 34g,   Sugars: 23g,   Fibre: 1g,

Protein: 5g,   Low in salt: 0.08g

33. Lemon Curd Pots

Preparation Time: 5 mins

Serves: 4

Ingredients:

- 300g jar lemon curd
- 100ml/3½ fl oz double cream
- 1 small block dark chocolate
- biscuits to serve, try shortbread or biscotti

Directions:

Take four small freezer-proof pots or ramekins and divide the lemon curd between them. Top with the cream, grate some chocolate over and place the pots in the freezer until well chilled. Serve with biscuits of your choice on the side.

Nutrition:

Kcal 404,   Low in salt: 0.14g,   Fat: 21g,

Saturates: 10g,   Carbs: 56g,   Fibre: 0.5g,

Sugars: 39.2g,   Protein: 2g

34. Rice pudding

Preparation Time: 5 mins

Cooking Time: 2 hrs

Serves: 4

Ingredients:

- 100g pudding rice
- butter, for the dish
- 50g sugar
- 700ml semi-skimmed milk
- pinch of grated nutmeg or strip lemon zest
- 1 bay leaf, or strip lemon zest

Directions:

Heat the oven to 150C/130C fan/gas 2. Wash and drain the rice. Butter a 850ml baking dish, then tip in the rice and sugar and stir through the milk. Sprinkle in the nutmeg and top with the bay leaf or lemon zest. Cook for 2 hrs or until the pudding wobbles ever so slightly when shaken.

Nutrition: per serving (using semi-skimmed milk)
Kcal 214, Low in salt: 0.2g, Protein: 8g, Sugars: 21g
Fat: 3g,   Saturates: 2g,   Carbs: 40g, Fibre: 0g

35. Self-Saucing Sticky Toffee Chocolate Pudding

Preparation Time: 20 mins

Cooking Time: 40 mins, plus 30 mins soaking

Serves: 8 – 10

Ingredients:

- 200g pitted medjool dates
- 100g unsalted butter, softened, plus extra for the dish
- 75g demerara sugar
- 75g dark brown soft sugar
- 2 large eggs
- 250g plain flour
- 1 tsp bicarbonate of soda
- 1 tbsp baking powder
- 100g dark chocolate, roughly chopped
- vanilla ice cream or custard, to serve

For the sauce:

- 200ml double cream
- 75g unsalted butter, cubed
- 200g dark brown soft sugar
- 30g cocoa powder

Directions:

Put the dates in a bowl and pour in 300ml boiling water. Leave to soak for 30 mins. Meanwhile, make the sauce by tipping all the ingredients, a big pinch of salt and 300ml boiling water into a pan, then whisk over a medium heat and simmer for 2 mins. Pour into a jug and leave to cool slightly. Once the dates are soaked, use a hand blender to blitz the dates and water until you have smooth paste. Leave to cool slightly. Butter a deep 35 x 25cm dish. Heat oven to 180C/160C fan/gas 4. Beat together the butter and sugar for 3 mins until smooth. Add the eggs, one at a time, beating between each addition. Fold in the flour, bicarb and baking powder along with a pinch of salt. Once combined, mix in the date purée, then fold in the dark chocolate. Pour the sponge batter into the prepared dish and spread out evenly using the back of a spoon. Pour the chocolate sauce evenly over the top of the batter. Bake in the oven for 30-35 mins until risen, then leave to rest for 2 mins. Serve warm with a big scoop of ice cream or warm custard.

Nutrition:

Kcal 604, Fat: 32g, Saturates: 19g, Salt: 0.7g, Carbs:72g, Sugars:50g, Fibre:4g, Protein: 7g,

36. Sticky Toffee Pudding

Preparation Time: 20 mins

Cooking Time: 2 hrs and 35 mins, plus cooling

Serves: 12

Ingredients:

- 250g dates, pitted and finely chopped
- 100g raisins
- 200ml golden or spiced rum
- 150g butter, softened, plus extra for the basin
- 50g light muscovado sugar
- 3 large eggs, beaten
- 375g self-raising flour
- ½ tsp mixed spice
- 1 tsp ground cinnamon
- 50ml milk

- vanilla custard or ice cream, to serve

For the toffee sauce:

- 75g light muscovado sugar
- 2 tbsp treacle
- 2 tbsp golden syrup
- 75g butter
- 150ml double cream

Directions:

Put the dates, raisins, rum and 100ml water in a small saucepan and set over a low heat until steaming, about 5 mins (or do this in the microwave). Leave to cool. Meanwhile, make the toffee sauce. Put all the ingredients except the cream in a small pan and bring to a simmer. Cook until the sugar has dissolved and the sauce is glossy, about 5 mins. Pour in the cream and cook for 2 mins more, stirring continuously, then remove from the heat and set aside. The sauce will continue to thicken as it cools. Generously butter a 1.5-litre pudding basin. Beat the butter and sugar until well combined in a large bowl using an electric whisk, or in a stand mixer. Add the eggs one at a time, beating well between each addition. Fold in the flour, spices and the soaked fruit until evenly incorporated, then stir in the milk. Pour a quarter of the toffee sauce into the base of the prepared basin, then spoon in the sponge batter. Place a sheet of baking parchment over a sheet of foil, then make a pleat in the centre. Use this to cover the pudding, parchment-side down, and tie securely under the lip of the basin using kitchen string. Transfer the basin to a steamer. Alternatively, put an upturned plate in the base of a large pan, sit the basin on top, and half-fill the pan with water from the kettle so it goes halfway up the side of the basin. Cover and cook over a low heat for 2 hrs 35 mins, checking the water level every so often and topping up when needed. Check the sponge is ready by inserting a skewer into the middle. If it comes out clean, the sponge is cooked. If any uncooked batter clings to the skewer, continue steaming, then check again after about 20 mins. To serve, warm the remaining toffee sauce over a low heat, invert the sponge onto a serving plate, and pour over the warmed sauce. Serve with custard or ice cream.

Recipe tip:

You can make the pudding up to a week in advance. After it's steamed, remove the foil and baking parchment and leave to cool completely. Stack a fresh sheet of baking parchment over a fresh sheet of foil, pleat, and use to cover the pudding as before. Keep the pudding in the fridge or a cool, dry place for up to one week. To serve, steam for 1 hr until fully reheated. Cover the reserved sauce and keep in the fridge, then reheat fully over a low heat for about 5
mins before serving.

Nutrition:

Kcal 522g, Fat: 24g,   Saturates: 15g, Salt: 0.7g
Carbs: 58 g, Sugars: 35g, Fibre: 0g, Protein: 6g,

37.   Brookies

Preparation Time: 20 mins

Cooking Time: 55 mins, plus 30 mins chilling and cooling

Ingredients:

For the cookie layer:

- 120g unsalted butter, softened, plus extra for the tin
- 120g light brown soft sugar
- 100g dark muscovado sugar
- 1 large egg, plus
- 1 egg yolk
- 250g plain flour
- ½ tsp bicarbonate of soda
- 50g milk chocolate chunks

For the brownie layer:

- 185g unsalted butter
- 185g dark chocolate (at least 70% cocoa solids)
- 3 large eggs
- 1 tsp vanilla extract
- 275g golden caster sugar
- 50g cocoa powder
- 130g plain flour
- 50g milk chocolate chunks

Directions:

Butter a 23cm square cake tin and line with baking parchment. Heat the oven to 180C/160C fan/gas 4. First, make the cookie layer. Put the butter and both sugars in a bowl and beat with an electric whisk until just combined. Alternatively, do this in a stand mixer. Add the whole egg and egg yolk, and beat again until combined. Mix in the flour, ¼ tsp salt, the bicarbonate of soda and chocolate chunks. Press the cookie dough into the base of the prepared tin using the back of a spoon, then chill for 30 mins.

For the brownie layer, melt the butter and chocolate in a heatproof bowl over a pan of just simmering water, stirring until smooth and combined. Leave to cool slightly, about 10 mins. Whisk the eggs, vanilla and sugar together in a large bowl with an electric whisk until slightly thickened, about 3 mins. Fold the cooled chocolate and butter mixture through the beaten eggs with a large spoon until well combined.

Fold the buttery chocolate mixture, cocoa and flour together to combine. Spoon the brownie mixture over the cookie dough layer, dot with the chocolate chunks, and sprinkle with sea salt flakes, if you like. Bake in the centre of the oven for 50 mins-1 hr, or until a skewer inserted into the middle comes out with just a few crumbs clinging to it. Leave to cool completely in the tin before cutting into squares.

Nutrition:

Kcal 489,   Fat: 25g,   Fibre: 3g,   Salt: 0.3g
Carbs: 57g, Sugars: 37g, Protein: 7g, Saturates: 15g

38. Chocolate Orange Babka

Preparation Time: 40 mins

Cooking Time: 40 mins, plus 2 hrs 30 mins-3 hrs proving, 2 hrs chilling and cooling

Serves: 14 - 16

Ingredients:

- 100ml whole milk
- 550g strong white bread flour, plus extra for dusting
- 100g caster sugar
- 7g sachet fast-action dried yeast
- 4 large eggs, at room temperature
- 150g unsalted butter, at room temperature, cut into cubes

For the filling:

- 50g light brown soft sugar
- 30g cocoa powder
- 125g dark chocolate, finely chopped

- 100g unsalted butter, chopped

- 3 oranges, zested

For the syrup:

- 100g caster sugar

- 3 oranges, juiced (or use the juice of 2 oranges mixed with 25ml triple sec), plus 1 orange, zest peeled and finely sliced into strips

Directions:

Heat the milk in a small pan over a low heat until warm, but not hot. Set aside. Put the flour into the bowl of a stand mixer. Add ½ tsp salt to one side of the bowl and the sugar and yeast to the other. Mix each side into the flour with your hands, then using the dough hook attachment until fully combined.

Pour in the warm milk, then, with the mixer on medium, add the eggs one at a time. Keep mixing the dough for 10 mins until smooth, then gradually add the butter, one or two cubes at a time, until fully incorporated, about 5-8 mins. Scrape down the sides of the bowl – the dough will be very soft.

Scrape the dough into a large bowl, cover with a clean tea towel and leave to rise for 1 hr 30 mins-2 hrs until doubled in size. Once doubled, chill for 1 hr. Line a large baking sheet with baking parchment and set aside. To make the filling, put all the filling ingredients and a large pinch of sea salt flakes in a small saucepan over a low-medium heat, stirring continuously until everything has melted together. Transfer to a bowl, leave to cool completely, then transfer to the fridge and chill for 40 mins, stirring every 20 mins until the mixture has thickened but is still spreadable.

Remove the dough from the fridge, and roll out on a lightly floured surface to a roughly 70 x 40cm rectangle. Spread the filling evenly over the dough using a spatula or palette knife. With a shorter end closest to you, roll the dough up into a tight sausage. Transfer to a board, seam-side down, and cut in half across the length so you have two long pieces. Lay the two pieces out in front of you, parallel to one another, and cross them over each other along the length in a plait-like pattern. Curl into a circle and join the ends to make a wreath, then carefully transfer to the lined sheet. Cover with a tea towel and leave to rise for 1 hr until doubled in size. Heat the oven to 180C/160C fan/gas 4 and bake the babka for 35-40 mins until golden.

For the syrup, simmer the sugar, orange juice and zest over a high heat for 5-10 mins until thickened. Brush the babka with the warm syrup. Strain the candied orange zest and scatter over the babka. Serve warm, or leave to cool completely, then keep wrapped. Will keep wrapped at room temperature for up to three days.

Nutrition:

Kcal 393,   Fat: 19g,   Saturates: 11g,

Carbs: 46g,   Sugars: 19g,   Fibre: 3g,   Protein: 8g,

Salt: 0.1g

39. Espresso Martini Cheesecake

Preparation Time: 40 mins

Cooking Time: 10 mins, plus cooling and 24 hrs freezing

Serves: 12

Ingredients:

- 70g salted butter, plus extra for the tin
- 100g dark chocolate digestive biscuits
- 150g almond cantuccini or biscotti
- 150g dark chocolate, chopped
- 500g full-fat soft cheese
- 180g icing sugar
- 300ml double cream
- 30ml espresso or strong coffee
- 50ml coffee liqueur
- 1 tsp vanilla bean paste, or 1 vanilla pod, split and seeds scraped out

For the coffee syrup:

- 50ml coffee liqueur
- 50ml espresso or strong coffee
- 50g golden caster sugar

To serve:

- 200g soured cream

- 30g chocolate-coated coffee beans

Directions:

Butter a 20 x 25 x 4.5cm loose- bottomed cake tin or a roughly 23cm loose-bottomed square cake tin and line with baking parchment. Melt the butter in a pan over a low heat, then pour into a large bowl and set aside. Put the digestive biscuits and cantuccini or biscotti in a food processor and blitz to fine crumbs. Alternatively, put them in a sealed sandwich bag and bash to crumbs with a rolling pin. Tip into the bowl containing the butter and stir to combine. Transfer the buttery crumbs to the prepared tin and firmly press into the base. Chill for 30 mins, or freeze for 10 mins.

Melt the chocolate in a heatproof bowl set over a pan of simmering water, making sure the bottom of the bowl doesn't touch the water. Stir until smooth, then leave to cool to room temperature, about 15 mins.

Divide the soft cheese, icing sugar and double cream equally between two bowls. To one bowl, add the cooled melted chocolate and beat with an electric whisk until thick and creamy. To the second bowl, add the coffee, coffee liqueur and vanilla, and beat until thick and creamy, about 3-5 mins (the coffee mixture will not get quite as thick). Spoon the chocolate mixture over the biscuit base and level with a palette knife. Freeze for 30 mins, or until starting to firm up. Spoon over the coffee mixture, level the surface and return to the freezer for at least another 24 hrs. Will keep frozen, well covered, for up to two weeks.

On the day you want to serve the cheesecake, make the coffee syrup. Pour the coffee liqueur, coffee and sugar into a small saucepan. Bring to a simmer and cook for 5 mins, or until syrupy enough to coat the back of a spoon. Leave to cool completely.

Take the cheesecake out of the freezer 1 hr before serving. Once defrosted, the cheesecake will keep in the fridge for up to three days. Spread the soured cream over the top, drizzle with the coffee syrup, then scatter over the coffee beans. Cut into 12 squares and serve straightaway (after about 5 mins the syrup will crack the soured cream).

Nutrition:

Kcal 548,   Fat: 38g,   Saturates: 23g, Salt: 0.5g
Carbs: 40g, Sugars: 32g, Fibre: 2g, Protein: 6g,

40. Lemon Drizzle Sponge Pudding

Preparation Time: 15 mins

Cooking Time: 50 mins

Serves: 10

Ingredients:

- 250g soft butter, plus extra for the dish
- 380g caster sugar
- 4 eggs
- 250g self-raising flour
- 1 tsp baking powder
- 3 lemons, zested and juiced
- 2½ tbsp cornflour
- custard or cream, to serve

For the drizzle:

- 50g icing sugar
- 1 lemon, juiced and zested

Directions:

Heat the oven to 180C/160C fan/gas 4. Butter a 30 x 20cm deep baking dish. Put the butter and 250g caster sugar in a bowl and beat for 5 mins until pale and fluffy. Whisk in the eggs, then sieve over the flour and baking powder and fold in until you have a batter. Stir in the lemon zest, reserving a little for decoration.

Spoon the sponge batter into the dish and smooth over the top. Mix the lemon juice with the cornflour in a heatproof bowl to make a smooth paste. Mix the remaining 130g caster sugar with 300ml boiling water in a jug, pour over the cornflour mix and whisk until smooth. Pour this over the sponge. Bake for 45-50 mins until golden and set, and the sponge springs back when touched. While the pudding is baking, make the lemon drizzle. Mix the icing sugar with enough lemon juice (about half of it) to create a loose consistency. Drizzle over the sponge while it's still warm and decorate with the reserved lemon zest. Serve straightaway with cream or custard.

Nutrition:

Kcal 492,   Fat: 23g,   Saturates: 14g, Salt: 0.9g
Carbs: 66g,   Sugars: 43g, Fibre: 1g,   Protein: 5g,

41.   Red Velvet Cookies

Preparation Time: 20 mins

Cooking Time: 15 mins, plus chilling

Serves: 16-18

Ingredients:

- 175g soft salted butter
- 200g light brown soft sugar
- 100g caster sugar
- 1 large egg
- 2 tsp vanilla extract
- ½-1 tbsp red food colouring gel, depending on strength
- 225g plain flour
- 25g cocoa powder
- ½ tsp bicarbonate of soda
- 150g white chocolate chips or chunks

For the drizzle:

- 2 tbsp soft cheese
- 6 tbsp icing sugar

Directions:

Beat the butter and sugars together with an electric whisk until pale and fluffy. Beat in the egg, vanilla and food colouring until you have a bright red batter. Sieve over the flour, cocoa and bicarb. Fold everything together to make a stiff evenly-coloured dough, then fold in the chocolate chips. Put the dough on a sheet of baking parchment, fold the parchment over the dough and mould into a sausage shape about 6cm wide. Chill until ready to bake. Will keep for a week in the fridge or one month in the freezer.

Heat the oven to 190C/170C fan/gas 5. Cut the cookie dough into 1cm thick slices using a sharp knife and arrange on two large baking sheets lined with baking parchment well-spaced apart so they have room to spread in the oven. Bake in batches, keeping the unbaked cookies on the sheet in the fridge while the rest are baking. Bake in the middle of the oven for 13-15 mins until the cookies are crisp at the edges, but still soft in the centre. Leave to cool on the baking sheet for a few minutes, then transfer to a wire rack to cool completely. Beat the soft cheese in a small bowl to a loose consistency, then stir in the icing sugar. Use a piping bag or spoon to drizzle the icing over the cookies. Un-iced cookies keep for five days in an airtight container, or two days iced.

Nutrition:

Kcal 268,   Fat: 12g,   Saturates: 7g,   Carbs: 36g,
Sugars: 26g,   Fibre: 1g,   Protein: 3g,   Salt: 0.3g

42. Rhubarb & Custard Blondies

Preparation Time: 15 mins

Cooking Time: 55 mins

Serves: 12

Ingredients:

- 225g salted butter (or unsalted with a pinch of salt), plus extra for the tin
- 200g light brown soft sugar
- 100g caster sugar
- 150g plain flour
- 50g custard powder
- ½ tsp baking powder
- 3 medium eggs
- 250g white chocolate chips or white chocolate finely chopped
- 2 tsp vanilla extract

For the rhubarb & custard swirl:

- 200g rhubarb (frozen, or canned and drained is fine)
- 75g caster sugar
- pink or red food colouring (optional)
- 4 tbsp ready-made custard (from a carton is fine, or made up from powder)

Directions:

For the rhubarb & custard swirl, put the rhubarb and sugar in a wide pan with 2 tbsp water (omit the water if using canned rhubarb). Cook over a medium heat, stirring frequently for about 10 mins, until the rhubarb breaks down and turns jammy. Add a few drops of food colouring if you want a pink rhubarb swirl, but the flavour will still be great if you're using green-tinged rhubarb. Leave to cool. Heat the oven to 180C/160C fan/gas 4. Put the butter and both sugars into a pan and put over a low heat. Melt together until smooth and shiny, then remove from the heat, and leave to cool for 10 mins while you sieve the flour, custard powder and baking powder in a bowl. Butter a 20 x 30cm baking tin and line with baking parchment.

Beat the eggs into the cooled sugar and butter mixture, then fold in the dry ingredients until you have a smooth batter. Stir in 150g of the chocolate chips and the vanilla. Pour into the brownie tin, then use a teaspoon to swirl rhubarb compote on top of the batter. Add dollops of the custard, then swirl a skewer or cocktail stick through the compote to create a marbled pattern.

Bake for 35-40 mins until set and the edges are coming away from the sides of the tin, then leave in the tin to cool. Melt the remaining 100g chocolate in short blasts in the microwave or in a bowl set over a pan of simmering water. Use a spoon to drizzle the chocolate over the blondie in a zig-zag pattern. Cut into squares to serve. Will keep for three days in an airtight container, or freeze the squares individually.

Nutrition:

Kcal 464, Fat: 24g,   Saturates: 14g, Protein: 5g,

Carbs: 57g,   Sugars: 44g, Salt: 0.6g, Fibre: 1g,

43. Snowy Coconut Loaf Cake

Preparation Time: 20 mins

Cooking Time: 1 hr and 10 mins

Serves: 10

Ingredients:

- 185g butter softened, plus extra for the tin
- 185g coconut milk, whisked
- 250g caster sugar
- 250g self-raising flour
- 3 large eggs
- 1 tsp coconut extract (optional)
- 25g desiccated coconut

For the icing:

- 100g butter, softened
- 250g icing sugar
- 2 tbsp coconut milk
- ½ tsp coconut extract (optional)
- 25g coconut chips or desiccated coconut
- white chocolate truffles or large white sprinkles, to decorate (optional)

Directions:

Heat the oven to 180C/160C fan/gas 4. Butter a 900g loaf tin (ours measured 10 x 21 x 5cm) and line the base with a long strip of baking parchment that overhangs the sides. Put the butter, coconut milk, sugar, flour, eggs, coconut extract (if using) and desiccated coconut in a large bowl and beat with an electric whisk until combined. Scrape into the prepared tin and level the top with a spatula or the back of a spoon. Bake for 55 mins-1 hr, or until the cake is risen and golden brown and a skewer inserted into the middle comes out clean. If any wet cake mixture clings to the skewer, bake for another 5-10 mins, then check again. Leave to cool in the tin for 10 mins, then lift the cake out onto a wire rack, using the parchment to help you. Leave to cool completely. The cooled cake will keep in the freezer, well wrapped, for up to two months.

To make the icing, beat the butter, sugar, coconut milk and coconut extract, if using, in a bowl until smooth and creamy. Spread over the top of the cake using a palette knife or the back of a spoon, then scatter over a generous layer of coconut chips. Decorate with white chocolate truffle 'snowballs' or large white sprinkles, if you like.

Nutrition: Kcal 589, Fat: 32g, Saturates: 21g, Salt: 0.8g Carbs: 70g, Sugars: 51g, Fibre: 2g, Protein: 6g

44.   Boozy Bombe

Preparation Time: 20 mins

Cooking Time: 5 mins, plus freezing

Serves: 8

Ingredients:

- 100g raisin
- 100g sultana
- 85g pack dried cranberries
- 6 tbsp brandy
- 2 tbsp dark muscovado sugar
- 284ml pot double cream
- 1 tbsp icing sugar
- 100g frozen cranberry (keep them frozen)
- 600ml good-quality fresh vanilla custard
- brandy butter, to serve (optional)
- Cranberry brandy butter sauce
- 85g light muscovado sugar
- 175g butter
- 2 tbsp brandy
- 100g frozen cranberry

Directions:

Put the dried fruit into a large bowl, add 2 tbsp brandy and the sugar, then cover with cling film. Microwave on High for 2 mins until the sugar has melted and the fruit plumped up. Give it a stir, then leave to cool and soak overnight. If you're short of time, carry on with step 2 and leave to soak for as long as it takes to complete step 2. Put the cream, remaining brandy and icing sugar into a large bowl and whip to soft peaks. Pour the custard into another bowl and fold the cream into it. Tip into a freezer container and freeze the mix for 4 hrs, stirring the frozen edges into the rest of the mixture every hour or so until the whole tub is soft, but frozen (or use an ice cream machine, churning for 20-30 mins until thick). Meanwhile, line a 1.2-litre pudding basin with cling film. Once the ice cream mix is thick, quickly fold the soaked fruit (and any liquid from it) and frozen cranberries through it and spoon into the lined basin. Freeze overnight or for at least 6 hrs. To serve, leave bombe at room temperature for 10 mins and turn out onto a serving plate. To make the cranberry brandy butter sauce, in a heavy-based pan gently heat muscovado sugar and butter until the sugar dissolves. Splash in brandy, add cranberries and boil gently till the cranberries pop, but still hold their shape and colour the sauce. If you want to, sieve the seeds out of the sauce and add some more cranberries for a really glossy finish. Serve hot or warm.

Nutrition:

Kcal 411,   Fat: 24g,   Saturates: 14g,

Carbs: 43g, Sugars: 40g, Fibre: 1g, Protein: 3g,   Low in salt: 0.14g

45. Black Forest Fool

Preparation Time: 10 mins

Serves: 6

Ingredients:

- 500ml double cream
- ½ tsp vanilla extract
- 2 tbsp icing sugar
- 250g Christmas cake or rich fruitcake
- 390g jar of black cherries in kirsch, drained, reserving the liquid for drizzling
- 50g dark chocolate , chopped

Directions:

Whisk the cream with the vanilla and icing sugar until it just holds its shape. Crumble the cake into six glasses, then top with a few cherries, a dollop of cream and a drizzle of the kirsch. Scatter over the chopped chocolate. A simple, quick and indulgent dessert you can rustle up in 10 minutes. If you want to make a non-alcoholic version, use a can of cherries in syrup instead.

Nutrition:

Kcal 682, Fat: 53g,   Saturates: 32g, Salt: 0.3g

Carbs: 45g, Sugars: 26g, Fibre: 2g,   Protein: 4g

46. Triple Chocolate & Peanut Butter Layer Cake

Preparation Time: 45 mins

Cooking Time: 30 mins - 1 hr, plus cooling and 1 hr 40 mins chilling

Serves: 14

Ingredients:

- 225ml rapeseed oil, plus more for the tins
- 250g self-raising flour
- 4 tbsp cocoa
- 1 ½ tsp bicarbonate of soda
- 225g caster sugar
- 3 tbsp golden syrup
- 3 large eggs, beaten
- 225ml milk

For the pretzel bark:

- 200g dark chocolate, chopped
- 2 tbsp chocolate chips
- small handful pretzel pieces
- 2 tbsp honeycomb pieces

For the icing:

- 65g dark chocolate

- 250g soft salted butter

- 500g icing sugar

- 45g smooth peanut butter

- 1-2 tbsp cocoa

For the ganache drip:

- 200ml double cream

- 100g dark chocolate, finely chopped

For the decoration:

- chocolate eggs, some hollow, some filled, gold lustre, toffee popcorn and pretzels

Directions:

Heat oven to 180C/160C fan/gas 4. Oil and line the base of three 19cm sandwich tins. Mix the flour, cocoa, bicarb and sugar in a bowl. Make a well in the centre and beat in the syrup, eggs, oil and milk with an electric whisk until smooth. Divide the mix between the tins, and bake for 25-30 mins until the cakes are risen and firm to the touch. Cool in the tins for 10 mins before turning out onto a cooling rack and cooling completely. At this stage, they can be frozen, well wrapped, for up to eight weeks. Make the bark while the cake is cooling. Melt the chocolate in short bursts in the microwave, stirring every 20 secs, until smooth. Spoon onto a parchment-lined baking tray and smooth over with a spatula to make a thinnish layer, around 35 x 20cm. Sprinkle over the chocolate chips along with the pieces of pretzel and honeycomb, then chill until solid. Remove the bark from the fridge and leave for a minute to come to room temperature before using a sharp knife to cut it into shards (if it's fridge cold, the chocolate will snap rather than cut). Chill again until you're ready to decorate the cake. To make the icing, melt the chocolate in the microwave, stirring between short blasts, then leave to cool a little. Meanwhile, beat the butter, icing sugar and 1 tbsp boiling water with an electric whisk or stand mixer, slowly at first, then turn up the speed and beat until you get a pale, fluffy icing. Spoon out a third of the mix into a separate bowl and stir in the peanut butter. Whisk the melted chocolate into the remainder of the icing, then beat in the cocoa if you want a darker, more chocolatey-coloured icing. Sandwich the three cakes together with the peanut butter icing. Use half the chocolate icing to coat the sides and top of the cake and fill in the edges between the layers, scraping off any excess. Chill for 20 mins. This is called a crumb coating, allowing you to get a really smooth finish when it comes to the final icing.

Spread the remaining chocolate icing over the lightly chilled cake, smoothing over the sides and top so you get a neat finish. Chill again for 20 mins. To make the ganache, heat the cream in a small pan until steaming. Tip the dark chocolate into a bowl, then pour over the cream. Mix well until smooth and shiny. Transfer to a piping bag and leave to cool for a few mins at room temperature. Pipe the ganache on top of the cake, nudging it over the edge and allowing it to drip down neatly. Do this all the way round the cake, then fill in the centre with more ganache. Smooth the top with a knife. Chill for 1 hr for the ganache to set. Press the bark shards into the cake, sticking up. Add lots of chocolate eggs, popcorn and pretzels in and around the shards.

Cut into slices to serve. Will keep for up to three days kept in a cool place in an airtight container.

<u>*RECIPE TIPS*</u> <u>BAKING IN BATCHES:</u>

If you don't have three cake tins, bake the sponges in batches, cleaning and drying the tin in between each one. You can use an 18cm tin if you don't have 19cm tins, just bake each cake for 5 mins more.

Nutrition:

Kcal 870,   Fat: 54g,   Saturates: 23g,   Salt:1g,

Carbs: 85g,   Sugars: 68g,   Fibre: 4g,   Protein:8g

47.　Easy Chocolate Molten Cakes

Preparation Time: 15 mins

Cooking Time: 20 mins

Serves: 6

Ingredients:

- 100g butter, plus extra to grease
- 100g dark chocolate, chopped
- 150g light brown soft sugar
- 3 large eggs
- ½ tsp vanilla extract
- 50g plain flour
- single cream, to serve

Directions:

Heat oven to 200C/180C fan/gas 6. Butter 6 dariole moulds or basins well and place on a baking tray. Put 100g butter and 100g chopped dark chocolate in a heatproof bowl and set over a pan of hot water (or alternatively put in the microwave and melt in 30 second bursts on a low setting) and stir until smooth. Set aside to cool slightly for 15 mins. Using an electric hand whisk, mix in 150g light brown soft sugar, then 3 large eggs, one at a time, followed by ½ tsp vanilla extract and finally 50g plain flour. Divide the mixture among the darioles or basins. You can now either put the mixture in the fridge, or freezer until you're ready to bake them. Can be cooked straight from frozen for 16 mins, or bake now for 10-12 mins until the tops are firm to the touch but the middles still feel squidgy. Carefully run a knife around the edge of each pudding, then turn out onto serving plates and serve with single cream.

Nutrition:

Kcal 391,   Fat: 24g,   Saturates: 14g,   Protein: 6g,

Salt: 0.5g,   Carbs: 36g,   Sugars: 28g,   Fibre: 2g,

48. Mango & Coconut Trifles

Preparation Time: 50 mins

Cooking Time: 15 mins, plus 3 hrs chilling and cooling

Serves: 4

Ingredients:

- 3 gelatine leaves
- 50ml orange juice
- 250g canned mango pulp
- 8 sponge fingers
- 4 tsp dark rum
- 1 ripe mango, halved, peeled and sliced
- 16 fresh or frozen raspberries
- 400ml can coconut milk
- 600ml double cream

- 1 tsp vanilla extract
- 3 egg yolks
- 80g caster sugar
- 1 tbsp cornflour
- 3 tbsp milk
- 80g coconut flakes
- 1 lime, zested

Directions:

Put the gelatine in a bowl, cover with cold water and leave to soak for 10 mins. Meanwhile, warm the orange juice in a small pan over a low heat. Squeeze the water from the gelatine, then whisk into the juice over the heat until the gelatine has dissolved. Don't let the mixture bubble, or the jelly won't set. Stir in the mango pulp until combined. Divide the sponge fingers between four dessert glasses, breaking to fit if needed, and press into the bases. Pour over the rum, then add a few mango slices and four raspberries each. Spoon the jelly mixture into the glasses so the fruit and sponges are covered. Chill for 2 hrs until set. Meanwhile, heat the coconut milk in a saucepan over a medium heat, stirring continuously until reduced by about a third. Whisk in half the cream and all the vanilla, then bring everything to a simmer. Mix the egg yolks with 50g sugar, the cornflour and milk in a large heatproof bowl until smooth. Slowly pour in the hot coconut cream while whisking to incorporate. Return to the saucepan over a medium-low heat, stirring for 5-7 mins until you have a thick but pourable custard. Remove from the heat, pour into a bowl and cover the surface with baking parchment. Leave to cool completely, then chill for at least

1 hr, or up to 24 hrs. Pour the custard over the set jellies and chill for another 2 hrs. Heat the oven to 160C/140C fan/gas 5. Sprinkle the coconut flakes over a baking sheet and bake for 4 mins, or until just toasted. Whip the remaining cream with the rest of the sugar to soft peaks using an electric whisk and spoon over the custard layer. Sprinkle over the lime zest and toasted coconut. Will keep chilled for up to 24 hrs.

Nutrition:

Kcal 925,   Fat: 77g,   Saturates: 51g,   Salt: 0.34g
Carbs: 44g,   Sugars: 34g,   Fibre: 3g,   Protein: 9g,

49.   Mango Sorbet

 Preparation Time: 15 mins, plus freezing

 Serves: 8

Ingredients:

- 3 large, ripe mangoes
- 200g caster sugar
- 1 lime , juiced

Directions:

Peel the mangoes with a vegetable peeler, cut as much of the flesh away from the stone as you can, put it in a food processor or blender. Add the sugar, lime juice and 200ml water. Blend for a few minutes, until the mango is very smooth and the sugar has dissolved – rub a little of the mixture between your fingers, if it still feels gritty, blend for a little longer. Pour into a container and put in the freezer for a few hours. Scrape the sorbet back into the blender (if it's very solid, leave at room temperature for 5-10 mins first). Whizz until you have a slushy mixture, then pour back into the tin and freeze for another hour or so. Repeat step. Freeze until solid (another hour or two). Will keep covered in the freezer for three months.

Nutrition:

Kcal 184,   Low in fat: 1g,   Saturates: 0.1g,

Carbs: 43g, Sugars: 43g, Fibre: 2g, Protein: 1g,

Salt: 0.01g

50. Chocolate & Peanut Butter Pavlova

![icon] **Preparation Time:** 45 mins

![icon] **Cooking Time:** 1 hr and 5 mins, plus cooling

![icon] **Serves:** 10-12

Ingredients:

For the dark chocolate crémeux:

- 75g whole milk
- 115ml whipping cream
- 2 egg yolks, reserving the whites for the meringue
- 50g caster sugar
- 150g dark chocolate, finely chopped
- 60g salted butter, softened

For the meringue:

- 3 large egg whites

- 200g caster sugar

- 1 tsp white wine vinegar

- 2 tsp cornflour

- 50g dark chocolate, melted and cooled

For the candied peanuts:

- 100g shelled peanuts, regular or roasted

- 60g granulated sugar

For the peanut butter cream:

- 100g white chocolate, roughly chopped

- 100g smooth peanut butter

- 25g cold salted butter, cut into cubes

- 225ml double cream

- dark chocolate shavings, to serve (optional)

Directions:

First, make the crémeux. Bring the milk and cream to the boil in a small saucepan, whisking occasionally. Whisk the egg yolks and sugar together in a medium heatproof bowl until smooth. Pour in the hot cream mixture in a steady stream, whisking continuously until combined. Return to the saucepan, and simmer over a low heat for 3-4 mins, stirring continously until thickened to a custard. Put the dark chocolate into a large heatproof bowl and strain the hot custard over it through a fine mesh sieve, whisking until the chocolate has melted and the mixture is smooth. Leave to cool for 5 mins until just warm. Add the butter and blitz using a hand blender until smooth. Cover and leave at room temperature until needed. Heat the oven to 150C/130C fan/gas 2 and line two baking sheets with baking parchment. For the meringue, beat the egg whites in a large, clean bowl using an electric whisk or in a stand mixer until soft peaks form, then gradually beat in the sugar, 1 tsp at a time, until the meringue is thick and glossy. Whisk in the vinegar and cornflour. Spoon half the meringue mixture into the middle of one of the prepared baking sheets, and spread out into a roughly 20-25cm circle. Repeat with the the remaining meringue mixture on the second baking sheet. Drizzle the melted chocolate evenly over both circles, then gently swirl it using a cutlery knife or skewer until you have a marbled effect. Bake for 1 hr, turn off the oven and leave the meringues to cool completely inside. Meanwhile, make the candied peanuts. Tip the peanuts, sugar and 1 tbsp water into a heavy-bottomed saucepan and cook over a medium heat for 3-4 mins, stirring until the peanuts start to crystallise and turn white. Continue to cook, stirring, for another 3-4 mins until the peanuts turn dark brown. Sprinkle with a pinch of sea salt flakes, then scrape onto a sheet of baking parchment. Spread out using a spatula, and leave to cool completely. For the peanut butter cream, melt the white chocolate, peanut butter, butter and 25ml cream in a small saucepan over a low heat, stirring until smooth. Transfer to a bowl and leave to cool for 10 mins. Whisk the remaining cream to soft peaks, then fold in the peanut butter mixture until thick and billowy. To assemble, put one meringue circle on a serving plate, spoon over half the crémeux followed by half the peanut butter cream, then sprinkle with half the candied peanuts. Top with the second meringue circle, then the remaining crémeux and peanut butter cream, and the rest of the candied peanuts. Scatter over some dark chocolate shavings, if you like. Will keep chilled for up to two days.

Nutrition:

Kcal 548,	Fat: 39g,	Saturates: 20g,
Carbs: 40g,	Sugars: 36g,	Fibre: 2g,
Protein: 9g,		Salt: 0.3g

51. Peanut Butter Cheesecake

Preparation Time: 8hours & 15 minutes

Cooking Time: 2 hours & 5 minutes

Serves: 16

Ingredients:

For Chocolate Cake:

- 1 ¾ cup all-purpose flour
- 1 cup buttermilk
- 2 teaspoon baking soda
- Heaping ¾ cup of cocoa
- 2 cup sugar
- 1 tablespoon vanilla extract
- 2 eggs room temp
- 1 cup black coffee hot
- ½ cup butter melted
- 1 teaspoon salt

For Cheesecake:

- 12 fun-sized Reese's Peanut Butter cups; chopped
- 1 ¼ cup sugar
- 4 packages full-fat cream cheese (8ounces each), softened
- ½ cup sour cream
- 5 large eggs, organic

- 1 can of dulce de leche (14ounces)
- 2 teaspoon vanilla extract

For Peanut Butter Buttercream:

- 4-5 cups powdered sugar
- 1 ½ teaspoon vanilla
- ¾ cup each of butter, peanut butter & shortening

For Ganache:

- 1 cup heavy cream
- 2 cups semi-sweet chocolate chips
- 1 teaspoon vanilla

Directions:

For the Chocolate Cake:

Line the bottoms of 2 round baking pans, 9" each with the parchment paper; coat it lightly with the cooking spray; set aside and then preheat your oven to 350 F in advance. Combine the flour together with baking soda, cocoa, sugar & salt in a large bowl; mix well. Slowly add in the eggs followed by the butter, buttermilk & vanilla; continue to mix after each addition until completely smooth. Fold in the hot coffee and mix until a runny batter form. Pour the prepared batter into the baking pans & bake in the preheated oven for 30 to 35 minutes. Remove from the oven & let cool in the pans for approximately 10 minutes then invert them onto the cooling racks. Once completely cool, wrap in the saran wrap & refrigerate.

For the Cheesecake:

Preheat your oven to 475 F. Fill large pan with approximately ½" of water & lightly coat a standard-sized spring-form pan, 9" with the non-stick cooking spray; wrap the bottom in a tinfoil. Combine the cream cheese using an electric mixer in a large bowl until completely fluffy. Add in the sugar, vanilla, and sour cream; continue to mix until combined well. Slowly mix in the eggs (ensure that you blend well after every addition) and then fold in the chopped Reese's Peanut Butter Cups. Pour into your prepared pan & place the pan in water dish. Bake in the preheated oven for 10 minutes; decrease the heat settings to 350 & continue baking until the cheesecake is just set, for 50 to 60 more minutes. Remove from the oven & let cool. Once done; cover & let refrigerate for overnight. Once cooled; trim off approximately ½ to 1" of the tops of the cheesecake to make level & then split the cake in half using a serrated knife or cake leveler. Let chill in a refrigerator until ready for use. Now prepare the peanut butter-butter cream by creaming the butter together with shortening; once fluffy, immediately add in the vanilla & peanut butter. Adding one cup at a time; add in the powdered sugar and continue to cream until you get your desired level of consistency; set aside. Add dulce de leche to a large bowl & add some teaspoons of the milk to thin out.

To Assemble:

Add 1 of your layers of chocolate cake either on a cake or turntable stand & top with half of the dulce de leche. Top the dulce de leche with a layer of cheesecake. Spread with approximately a cup of the peanut butter-butter cream & top with a layer more of cheesecake. Spread the leftover dulce de leche & top with a layer of cake as well. Trip the outside of cake, if required and make it even & spread a thin layer of your peanut butter-butter cream to do a crumb coating and seal any spaces or gaps in the cake. Place in the freezer until slightly harden up, for half an hour. In the meantime, prepare the ganache. Add the chocolate chips to heat proof bowl & add in the heavy cream to the saucepan; heat until it just begins to boil, over moderate heat. Pour the cream on top of the chocolate chips; cover for 5 to 7 minutes. Remove the cover & stir until the chocolate completely melted into the cream. Let sit until slightly thickens. Remove the cake from freeze & pour some of the ganache on top and spread down the sides of your cake. Repeat until sides and top of cake are completely covered. Place ¼ cup of the peanut butter in small bowl & heat for a couple of minutes (over medium-low heat), until liquid then drizzle on top of the cake. Carefully decorate the bottom and top of your cake with the leftover buttercream.

Nutrition:

Calories: 592,   Total Fat: 42g,   Sugar: 32g,
Cholesterol: 138mg, Sodium: 436mg,   Protein: 12
Potassium:270mg,   Total Carbs:45g,
Dietary Fiber:1.5g

CPSIA information can be obtained
at www.ICGtesting.com
Printed in the USA
BVHW091923060521
606647BV00004B/674